When Moms Divorce

written + illustrated by
SARA OLSHER

mighty + bright

Hi, my
name is Mia!

And this is Stuart. Stuart feels better when he knows what's going to happen every day.

(Actually, **everybody** feels better when they know what's going to happen - even grown-ups!)

Most of the time we do the same things in the mornings. We wake up.

We eat breakfast.
(I like apples.
Stuart only eats bugs.)

Usually nights are the same too. We brush our teeth.

Open your mouth, Stuart!

We put on jammies, and we go to bed. Every day ends with sleep.

But our days can be different.

Some days we go to school, and some days are the weekend!

When something big changes, what we do each day can change too. Stuart wants to know what happens to our days when our parents get a **divorce**.

But he doesn't really understand what divorce is - do you?

Divorce is when parents decide not to be married anymore, and they live in two different houses.

Hearing this makes Stuart upset.
He wants to know —
what's going to happen?
What about me?

At first, divorce can be confusing or scary for kids.
After all, you can't be in two houses at the same time.

Some kids worry that they caused their parents to get a divorce,
especially if the parents argue about the kids. Kids making mistakes is not
why parents get divorced. Divorce is never, ever a kid's fault. Divorce is
always about the parents' problems with each other, **never** about their kids.

Did I do something wrong?

When parents divorce they move into two different houses, and things change for everyone in the family.

Or a treehouse?

...what about me? Where do I go?

Sometimes each parent gets a new place to live, and sometimes only one does.

The kids spend some of the time at one house, and some of the time at the other house.

Some kids spend the **same amount of time** with each parent. Other kids live with **one parent most of the time** and visit the other parent. Every family is different.

Your parents can use a calendar to
show you when you'll see each parent.

Some days, you go to sleep in the same
house you woke up in. Other days,
you might wake up at one house
and go to sleep at the other house.

Divorce might make you feel some really big feelings.
You might get angry or sad or worried because it's different now,
and you're wondering if it's different **good** or different **bad**.

It might be a little bit of both.

There are some good things about divorce.
First, after a divorce parents don't fight as much, which means
they're happier and can be more fun to be around.

Two houses also means that kids get two bedrooms, two sets of toys, and
even two toothbrushes - which can be fun!

There are also some not-so-great things about divorce.

When you are with one parent, you might miss your other parent.
When this happens, come up with a plan for when you can talk to them on the phone or see their face, and look at your calendar for when you'll see them next.

Another not-very-fun thing about divorce is that sometimes parents don't get along. Sometimes they get mad at each other and can't agree on things.

That can be hard for kids, and sometimes you might feel like you're in the middle, which is no fun at all. Everyone — including your parents — hopes that will change.

It might take awhile for them to get along, but hopefully they can remember to be kind to each other.

The longer parents are divorced, the easier it is for them to get along.

Your family is going through something hard right now, but it **will** get so much easier.

...ely there's nothing you can do to fix your parents' marriage. ...se the divorce (that's impossible) and you can't stop it either.

...might feel like your family is broken. But it's not broken — ...now. And there is one **very** important thing to remember:

Even if your parents don't love each other the same way anymore, they will always love **you**. A parent's love for their kids is **forever**, and nothing you do, good or bad, can change that.

Some kids worry about their parents, and want to make sure they are okay. But grown-ups are grown up! It's their job to take care of their feelings **and** help you with yours.

Even though some things are changing,
lots of things will stay the same.

Every morning, you will wake up, and every night, you'll go to sleep.
Your parents will always be your parents, and they will always love you.

Stuart feels a lot better now that he knows what to expect.
Even though our days can be different, it helps to plan out our week
together so we know what's going to happen next.

There are a lot of fun things to look forward to, like
movie nights, sports, play dates, craft time,
and special time with each parent.

And remember, when things get hard it's important to share how you are feeling with a grown-up. By planning special time together, you have a time when you know it's okay to talk about your feelings . . . or anything else! **We can do hard things, together!**

More Help
Making Divorce Easier on Kids
from *mighty + bright*

Magnetic Charts Based on Decades of Science

. . . and featured in POPSUGAR, Reader's Digest, and more.

A divorce changes your family's routines, which is hard on kids. They need to know what to expect, and when — which is proven to decrease their anxiety levels.

Each set comes with enough magnets to display the vast majority of custody schedules: 5 of each parent, and two "transition" days, for days when you exchange the kids.

Learn more on our website: mightyandbright.com/divorce

Easily show kids when they'll see each parent, and when. Choose from mom + dad, two moms, or two dads.

Easily display other elements of your kids' schedules, such as sports or play dates.

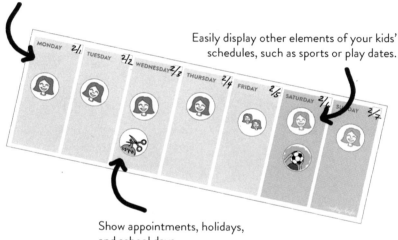

Show appointments, holidays, and school days.

Made in United States
Orlando, FL
01 August 2022